Following Rules at School

UNDERSTANDING CITIZENSHIP

Corina Jeffries

CIVICS FOR THE REAL WORLD™

Rosen Classroom™

Published in 2019 by The Rosen Publishing Group, Inc.
29 East 21st Street, New York, NY 10010

Book Design: Rachel Rising
Editor: Ryan Wolf

Photo Credits: Cover Syda Productions/Shutterstock.com; p. 4 ESB Professional/Shutterstock.com; p. 7 GagliardiImages/Shutterstock.com; p. 8 Sergiy Bykhunenko/Shutterstock.com; p. 11 TinnaPong/Shutterstock.com; pp. 12, 14 Monkey Business Images/Shutterstock.com.

ISBN: 9781538365571
6-pack ISBN: 9781538365588

Manufactured in the United States of America

CPSIA Compliance Information: Batch #WS18RC: For Further Information contact Rosen Publishing, New York, New York at 1-800-237-9932

Table of Contents

Everyone Has Rules

There are rules for everyone in the world. This is true for both kids and adults. You might think there are too many rules for you when you're young. However, there are reasons for these rules.

Many rules are meant to keep you safe and make sure you can learn. This is very true for rules at school.

School Rules

Every school has different rules. Many of these rules might be **similar**. Usually, you can't run in the hallways. You can't talk while your teacher is talking. You have to show respect for adults in school. And you can't bother your classmates while they're trying to learn. Sometimes, though, there are special rules because of the **circumstances** at a school.

Different Circumstances

A school in a snowy area might have a rule about not wearing messy, snow-covered boots in the gym or in classrooms. People could slip on the mess!

A school where there are many students with a peanut **allergy** might choose to ban peanut butter. Even if you don't like these rules, they're there to keep people safe and make sure they can learn.

For Safety's Sake

Think about the reasons for rules at your school. Why can't you run in the hallways? It's fun! But if you run, you might slip or run into other people. You could get hurt or they might be hurt. If your school has a playground, there are probably rules about that, too. You have to be careful and use the **equipment** in the correct manner.

wall

Listening, Learning

Some rules are there to make sure there are conditions in which all students can learn. Why can't you talk to your friends during a lesson? It's fun! But if you're talking, your friends and other students can't hear the teacher. You can't hear the teacher either! You're not learning. You and others go to school to learn things you need to know.

Make a Difference

Sometimes you might think a rule at school is unfair. If you learn more about it and still think it's unfair, talk to your teacher or principal about it. Maybe they'll consider changing it or give you more **information** about why the rule exists.

You might also have an idea for a new rule that will help people. Tell your teacher if you do!

Glossary

allergy: A bad bodily reaction to certain foods, animals, or surroundings.

circumstances: A condition or fact that affects something.

equipment: Tools, clothing, and other items used to do something

information: Facts about a subject.

similar: Almost the same as something else.

Index